Outside the Frame

New and Selected Poems

Marilyn L. Taylor

KELSAY BOOKS
~ 2021 ~

Text copyright © 2021 Marilyn L. Taylor

The Library of Congress has assigned
this edition a Control Number of
2021949977

ISBN ISBN: 978-1-63980-070-4 (paperback)

Cover image: *Manganese Falls, Copper Harbor* by Hans Isaacson, unsplash.com

Cover and book design by F. J. Bergmann

Kelsay Books
502 S 1040 E
A119
American Fork, Utah 84003
kelsaybooks.com

First Printing

I extend my deepest appreciation to the many extraordinary poets who have helped and guided me along the way to this collection, particularly Dick Allen, Jeannie Bergmann, Peggy Bresnahan, Kim Bridgford, Debra Bruce, Thomas Cable, Barbara Crooker, and Robert Siegel.

Table of Contents

I.

The Aging Huntress Speaks to Her Reflection	3
If, in October	4
Home Again, Home Again	5
Family Picnic	6
From a Dark Place	7
In Other News	8
Iron Man	9
Sestina for My Mother	10
Lonely as a Cloud	12
Notes from the Good-Girl Chronicles, 1963	13

II.

To the Four Who Would Be Will	23
The Agnostic's Villanelle	25
Piano Overture	26
Crickets: A Late Chorale	27
Drinking with Dylan Thomas	28
The Geniuses Among Us	29
A Double-Dactyl for Emily	30
Reading *Little Women* in 1962	31
Shostakovich's 5th Symphony	32
Sonnet in Defense of the Much-Maligned Spondee	33
Block That Trope	35

III.

Outside the Frame	39
After the Midnight Phone Call	51
The Blue Water Buffalo	53
For Lucy, Who Came First	54

Leaving the Clinic 55
What They Don't Know 56
Message from the Ice Cave 57

IV.

Reading the Obituaries 61
Late Spring, Early Fall 62
Family Dynamic 63
Women at Sixty 64
Aunt Eudora's Harlequin Romance 66
The Seventy-Somethings in the Workshop 67
The Tenth Avenue Care Home 68
Rondeau: Old Woman with Cat 70
Scaffolding 71
The Lovers at Eighty 72
We Real Old 73

V.

Along the Brule 77
Extravaganza at Dave's 78
The Amazing Perseverance of the Sand-Hill Crane 79
Summer Sapphics 80
Still Lives 81
Another Reason Never to Live North of 43 Degrees Latitude … 82
Tackiest of Trees 83
Drive All Night 84
No Two Exactly Alike 86
Snow Mist 87

VI.

A Highly Caloric Lament 91
Subject to Change 92
Always Questions 93

First Day in London	94
Genesis	95
To My Neighbor John, Who Is Completely Happy	96
For Max at Five Months	97
Cecelia and Bobby: A Tale of Love Gone Wrong	98
Another Thing I Ought to Be Doing	99
To a Cat Gone Blind in Her Nineteenth Summer	101
The Turban	102
In Tanzania	103
The Odalisques	104
The Gradual Unraveling of a Sycophant	105

VII.

The Day after I Die	109
Carpe Diem: A Quasi-Translation from the Latin	111
Notice from the Sweet Chariot Funeral Parlor	112
Contingency	113
To the Mother of a Dead Marine	114
At the End	115
Poem for a 75th Birthday	116
One by One	118
What Becomes of Us	120
Posthumous Instructions	121
Glimmers in a Time of Peril	122
Acknowledgments	123
About the Author	125

I.

The Aging Huntress Speaks to Her Reflection

Dear old moon of a face,
you've been looking back at me
for decades now
always giving me your best tilt
and a little quiver of lies—
but don't I love you for it?

Don't I fix my gaze on all
your nubbins and craters,
know your geography by heart?
Maybe I'll take you to town tonight,
tricked out in gilt and camouflage—
see how it goes with the men.

Not the young ones, those cheerful bucks
who look at you with all their teeth
thinking: *Teapot. Hairpin. Marianne Moore.*

It's their fathers, beery and balding,
and the loners in their silver ponytails,
heartbreakingly wistful—

they're the ones I want
to cool my heels with, feel
the warm breath of on my neck

while we knock a few back,
shoot the breeze, bathe together
in your fading borrowed light.

Marilyn L. Taylor

If, in October

I should be driving past a row
of brick-and-shingle bungalows
when maple leaves are sticking to the sidewalk
and a rain-glossed school bus starts to swing
its yellow bulk around the corner,

there you are again—framed in a wavy
leaded window, watering a long-fingered
philodendron while the Victrola
clatters out Landowska's version of
the *Little Preludes* through the glass

and I am nine years old—and you,
the center of my small universe,
are the love of my life, to whose powdered
presence I come home blissfully,
day after dangerous day

utterly innocent of a distant time
when you will turn from me
and withdraw into my archive of losses.
Even your quaint name, *Alice,* melts
to nearly nothing on my tongue.

Home Again, Home Again

The children are back, the children are back—
They've come to take refuge, exhale and unpack;
The marriage has faltered, the job has gone bad,
Come open the door for them, Mother and Dad.

The city apartment is leaky and cold,
The landlord lascivious, greedy and old—
The mattress is lumpy, the oven's encrusted,
The freezer, the fan, and the toilet have rusted.

The company caved, the boss went broke,
The job and the love-affair, all up in smoke.
The anguish of loneliness comes as a shock—
O heart in the doldrums, O heart in hock.

And so they return with their piles of possessions,
Their terrified cats and their mournful expressions,
Reclaiming the bedrooms they had in their teens,
Clean towels, warm comforter, glass figurines.

Downstairs in the kitchen the father and mother
Don't say a word, but they look at each other
As down from the hill comes Jill, comes Jack.
The children are back. The children are back.

Marilyn L. Taylor

Family Picnic

Life hasn't been easy for Betsy since she turned
thirteen—just look at her, the sniffy way
she sits all by herself, wincing with scorn
at her noisy cousins lining up to play
a pick-up softball game before the day
runs out. *Childish,* she mutters from the chair
in which she lounges, tossing back her hair.

But now, two uncles and a favorite aunt
are filling in at right field and third base;
Betsy's breathing quickens, but she can't
stop buffing her nails, sucking in her face,
keeping her careful distance—just in case
we take her for that splendid child Betsy,
who left us only very recently.

From a Dark Place

Who are you, little one, still floating
in my daughter's womb? I didn't know you
in my time, yet you look like me—
there is a flare to the nostril and a tinge
to the hair that is ours.

Your eyes are sealed like mine,
but your mouth opens and closes
with incipient messages—
and if I should whisper back
you would listen, spinning with delight.

Unfold your fingers, if you can—
they are waiting to grow eloquent
and strong. They will move under mine
the first time you touch the watered silk
of an iris, or your mother's face.

Your bed narrows, your bones
are bonding as mine fall
to powder. Soon we will glide away
from one another— you won't remember
passing me in the dissolving dark.

But you have my gifts:
the chromata of our past, strung jewels
I harbored for you all my life.
Without their weight, I vanish
just as you, moon-drenched, appear.

Marilyn L. Taylor

In Other News

They called the circumstances "drug-related"
when they found her—face-up, open-eyed,
bloody, but fully clothed. Witnesses said
the murdered girl had not been violated
—and you could call that lucky. Her first stroke
of luck since the convulsive day she fled
from the cold kitchen where her mother spread
her fury every morning, black and thick
for breakfast, making the corrupted air
unfit to breathe. Forcing her out the door.
I'll kill the little bitch her mother swore
when she comes crawling back from god-knows-where—
a comment the police chose to ignore,
because it hardly mattered anymore.

Iron Man

is what the nurses named you late last night
as your lungs kept steadily inflating,
hesitating—then deflating, right
on cue, your heart fixated on creating

a steady backbeat for the crusty rasp
of respiration. I saw how your hands
had interlaced themselves into the grasp
of one another—like the sweet demands

the dying lay on those already grieving.
Then I heard your bedside amaryllis
drop a wilted bloom—a sign you're leaving—
and found in that a cryptic kind of solace.

So keep on breathing, dear heart. We both know
it's not quite time—not yet—for you to go.

Marilyn L. Taylor

A Sestina for My Mother

We never mentioned dying, she and I;
never spoke of passing on, growing old
with grace, wearing lipstick to the last
emergency, all that. But she died. Because
of cigarettes, they said, but I knew better—
her inner fire, untended, guttered out.

When she lay sick, the news had not come out
about the changes (neither she nor I
had seen them coming). Not knowing any better,
we worried that she'd broken all the old
rules, flouted ancient customs, because
she hadn't done her penance first, her dying last.

But he's Attila, she hissed to me at last;
*he's Norman Bates, before they dragged him out
of the cellar. Benedict Arnold, because
he turned on me. He was Pinkerton, I
the idiot Butterfly. I'll stab the old
bastard through the heart when I get better.*

But she never did get better,
she got weaker, and her fury didn't last;
her face took on the thick sheen of old
ivory as she let herself run out
of time. She could not know that I
was dying too—the nice I, the I she knew—because

I seemed, next to her, so alive. Because
I was getting stronger, better,
even as she blurred and faded. Even as I
saw her breaking up, receding with the last
yellow shreds of the sun. Snuffed out.
But me, me—I'm rekindled by the old

fires. I burn. I have become the wicked old
witch. I am Grendel's mother, because
of her pain. I am the bat out
of Hell. I am Goneril, or better
still, Hecate. And with my wild torch, I
will light her way at last.

And you'd better not howl, old
man, or beg with your last shout—because
I'm coming, here I come, to cut your black heart out.

Marilyn L. Taylor

Lonely as a Cloud

So here they come,
one month to the day
after your funeral—
the goddamn daffodils
you planted last fall

Notes from The Good-Girl Chronicles, 1963

I. Reminiscences of a Fly-Girl

Back when the friendly skies were full of virgins,
I was one of them—naive, addled,
benighted as a parakeet emerging
from its covered cage. I'd been re-modeled:
my college pleats and plaids had been replaced
by a mock-military fitted suit
and soldier-cap—utterly chaste,
yet so erotic, so forbidden-fruit,
I was the concubine inside the head
of every traveling salesman on the plane.
He'd have me stripped and bouncing into bed
with him, bearing my bottles of champagne
with giggles and conspiratorial wink—
all this before I'd poured a single drink.

Marilyn L. Taylor

II. Porter Powell's Wife

All this, before I'd even poured his drink:
the swift removal of his coat, a match
to light his cigarette; a moist, pale pink
lipsticky kiss; one moment more to fetch
the *Wall Street Journal*. Then his Crown
Royal (rocks, splash, twist), a rack of lamb,
his monologue du jour (the putting down
of one more office coup) ad nauseam
while I provide encouraging remarks,
followed by my mentioning the bank
and how they called today about some checks
that didn't clear. I watch his eyes go blank.
He drops his fork, rises from his place
and slaps me, hard, three times across the face.

III. Celebrity's Mother

I've slapped myself three times across the face,
so I know it's not a dream, I swear—
my babygirl has really won first place
in the beauty pageant at State Fair.
Look how she slinks on those high heels,
cranks her little hips just like a pro
down that runway—honey, she's on wheels,
she's headed for the Johnny Carson show.
Come on, sweetheart, talk a little louder,
bat those lashes, lick your lips a lot;
make your poor old mama even prouder—
grab for what your mama never got.
Thank you, Jesus! Thank you, Maidenform!
Just watch my baby take the world by storm.

Marilyn L. Taylor

IV. Sixteen

I didn't want to take the world by storm—
just hoped to be a wife and mom someday,
but I've blown it all to kingdom come
because this boy and I went all the way.
I can't imagine what got into me
(except for him, of course) because I'm smart,
I know how boys will hold you close and cry
and make up stories that you take to heart
before they drop you like a shoe—and smirk
at you for buying into all their shit.
I guess I'm just another dirty joke,
a stupid nympho they can laugh about.
I never was a bargain anyhow,
but nobody would ever want me now.

V. George and Vera Carter's Wonderful Daughter

Nobody will ever want me more
than my sullen, shrinking parents do;
they think the very fact that I was born
proves I owe them both a thing or two.
So I've become the daughter that they crave—
a loyal and obedient retainer
who brings them what they need to stay alive
and well—from laxatives to Sunday dinner.
I listen to them re-arrange the past
to suit themselves (their favorite diversion)
and see to it they fall asleep at last,
allowing me an evening for submersion
in that alarming book I bought last week:
something called *The Feminine Mystique*.

Marilyn L. Taylor

VI. The Block-Watcher

You could call it a feminine mistake,
that thing my neighbor did—her moving out
like that. At night! She didn't even take
her clothes; just her hat and overcoat,
some books, and boom!—she's out the door.
Just drove away without a word to Bob—
because she knew he meant it when he swore
that he would never let her get a job.
I guess she thinks her fancy education
entitles her to some sort of "career,"
like that bunch from Women's Liberation
who bellyache and burn their underwear.
But if you ask me, she's acting like a brat,
throwing away her happiness like that.

VII. Mrs. McKinney Looks Back

I've thrown away my happiness, like that
old crone in the fairy tale. I'm frail
and shriveled now—and haunted by the thought
of what I might have been, had I been male:
I'd probably have taken center stage
in some exciting, world-altering dance.
But it's been such a stupefying age
for women. No one cared whether we flounced
or crawled through all the tragicomic phases
of our lives— we nearly always played
our grand theatricals to empty houses.
But I can't blame the men. They understood
the world was theirs, with all of its diversions—
just look: the skies are filled with friendly virgins!

II.

To the Four Who Would Be Will

Ah, gentlemen, you were a stellar quartet
of writers with copious talents, and yet
if you keep insisting, five centuries later,
that one of you had to be Falstaff's creator
as well as Cordelia's, and also Othello's,
you're quite a collection of devious fellows.

My Lord Francis Bacon, let's open with you:
a scholar you were, and a scientist too;
you wrote of enlightenment, back in the day—
but nary a poem, and never a play.
It's likely that we would be sadly mistaken
to look for a Hamlet along with our Bacon.

Sir Christopher Marlowe (known also as "Kit"),
you wrote some remarkable plays, we admit.
But why would you bother to fake your own death
so critics could claim that you'd written Macbeth
long after you died—like a playwright from hell?
And a hundred and fifty-four sonnets, as well?

And Sir William Stanley, you're trying too hard;
You're not the same William we know as the bard.
We know your initials are W. S.,
and you were a scoundrel—but nevertheless,
do not be surprised when we give you the bird
instead of the credit for *Richard the Third*.

So Edward de Vere, you're the final contender
and many insist you should never surrender,
since you were the one wearing velvet and laces
who romped in Verona and similar places.

Marilyn L. Taylor

You looked like a poet, you dressed fit to kill,
but no other threads ever linked you to Will.

Lord Bacon, Lord Stanley, Sir Marlowe, de Vere,
just what do you think you're accomplishing here?
Your conspiracy theories belong on the shelf,
but not on the one meant for Shakespeare himself.
Remember, he said, "To thine own self be true,"
which goes for us all—but especially you.

The Agnostic's Villanelle

She cannot fathom what God had in mind
or what eternal Truth was brought to bear
when Beethoven went deaf, and Milton blind.

Although she knows God will be disinclined
to answer her subversive little prayer,
she cannot fathom what He had in mind.

How many masterworks were left behind—
unwritten verses, music lost in air—
when Beethoven went deaf, and Milton blind?

Was God afraid of being undermined
by feats as near to the sublime as theirs?
If not, she can't tell what He had in mind

Unless He was incensed by humankind,
flinging back to Earth his own despair
when Beethoven went deaf, and Milton blind.

How will she bear it, should she find
no other answer but that God could err?
Can no one tell her what He had in mind
when Beethoven went deaf, and Milton blind?

Marilyn L. Taylor

Piano Overture

He came to our apartment twice a year
to tune my mother's piano. All day long
we tiptoed, trying not to interfere
with what to us were strange, unearthly songs.

He never struck a heavy, luscious chord—
only fifths, fourths, octaves—clean and spare;
brandishing his hammer like a sword,
we watched him wring concordance from the air.

Taut as pulled wire, he'd lean into the keys,
his practiced fingers pressing note on note,
hunting down aberrant harmonies
and any latent quaver in the throat.

At last the piano, gaping and undone,
its very heart exposed for all to see,
would wait in silence, chastened as a nun,
for the blasphemies of Chopin and Satie.

Crickets: A Late Chorale

As if Boulez had raised his arms
and readied his baton,
the crickets poise themselves to play
their autumn song.

Soprano saxophones invade
the saturated air
with rounds of semi-quavers, shrill
against the ear.

Repetitive cacophony
becomes the leitmotif—
they know their time to reproduce
is growing brief.

And we who listen will do one
of several likely things:
deny the deviousness of time,
or fold our wings

or open them impulsively,
chirping with all our mights
for one more spell—or maybe two—
of red-hot nights.

Marilyn L. Taylor

Drinking with Dylan Thomas

Tonight I'll grab a drink with Dylan Thomas.
How's that for a spectacular idea,
libidinous with fantasy and promise?

I'll slide into a pair of silk pajamas,
pour myself a glass of red sangria
and raise a toast to honor Dylan Thomas.

I'll sing his soulful songs and melodramas
(ah, that lilting onomatopoeia—
part Welsh, part fantasy, part promise)

and chant with him his childhood panoramas
tinged with the implicit paranoia
known as "quintessential Dylan Thomas."

I'll hear the stresses, stanza breaks and commas,
the architecture of his prosody—a
fantasy, foreshadowing a promise

in cadences he can't keep hidden from us.
So go ahead, call it a panacea,
libidinous with fantasy and promise—
but I'll still grab that drink with Dylan Thomas.

The Geniuses Among Us

They take us by surprise, these tall perennials
that jut like hollyhocks above the canopy
of all the rest of us—bright testimonials
to the scale of human possibility.
They come to bloom for every generation,
blazing with extraordinary notions
from the taproots of imagination—
dazzling us with incandescent visions.
And soon, the things we never thought would happen
start to happen: the solid fences
of reality begin to soften,
crumbling into fables and romances—
and we turn away from where we've been
to a new place, where light is pouring in.

Marilyn L. Taylor

A Double-Dactyl for Emily

Higgledy-piggledy,
Higginson's Dickinson
wrote in respectable meter and rhyme.
Nobody spotted the
proto-postmodernist
radical poetess, biding her time.

Reading *Little Women* in 1962

Of course I knew perfectly well that Alcott
wrote it ages and ages ago, when girls were
used to that kind of really dismal stuff—
But by chapter 36 it was pretty clear to me
that Beth was going to die (and really soon).
I couldn't stand it. "Louisa May!" I cried
from the depths of my soul, "How could you
do this? How could you kill her?"

And then I'd conjure up my own sister Pam
with her orange bangs and denim pedal-pushers
stretched out in a four-poster bed under a faded quilt.
She'd be way too weak for needlework by now,
so I'd bring her tea in a china cup and bend
over her counterpane (what's a counterpane, anyway?)
in my long, dark dress, crooning something
like "I Wanna Be Your Party Doll" and Pam
would shoot me a trembly smile and slurp some tea.

"Read me a story," she would beg, "to guide me
to the promised land." So I'd take my grimy copy
of *Tropic of Cancer* out of my pocket and read to her
from the best parts. She'd ask me to read some of them
again and again. Then she'd close her eyes
and we would speak quietly of the cute new boy
who'd moved into the house next door. His name
would be Laurie. And then she'd make me promise
that the minute she died I had to go over there
and ask him if he wanted to go to her funeral with me,
and take in a movie afterwards. Or a play, or
whatever they did in those days. And I would nod
bravely and say yes of course I would. Of course.

Marilyn L. Taylor

Shostakovich's 5th Symphony

Dmitri Shostakovich, when you wrote
the monumental score that came to be
your magnum opus—note by careful note—

had bitterness begun to fill your throat
with bile? Or did you feel some ecstasy,
Dmitri, when you clenched your fist and wrote

the fierce fourth movement, as if some remote
orchestra from a future century
would play it as your opus—every note

a metaphor? We're shaken when they quote
your fury with their pounding tympani,
Dmitri—how indelibly you wrote

your outrage in, with no attempt to sugar-coat
your leader's crimes against humanity.
With this, your magnum opus, every note

still hovers. You gave us an antidote
to subjugation and brutality,
Maestro Shostakovich, when you wrote
your magnum opus—note by wrenching note.

Sonnet in Defense of the Much-Maligned Spondee

> *Some poets and scholars believe that a true spondaic foot is impossible to achieve—that no two consecutive syllables can have the exact same weight or emphasis.*
> —Liz Wager, "A Look at the Spondee Metrical Foot"

No such foot exists in English,
    some say.
Tell them otherwise? They'll whistle
    No way.
Even if you're heading north to
    Green Bay—
Driving through a freezing blizzard
    all day,

Stuffed inside a green and yellow
    down coat
Fighting off a virus plus a
    sore throat,
They will still be adamant—but
    don't gloat.
Don't insist their hocus-pocus
    won't float.

Even though they know they may be
    all wet
Don't expect them to admit it.
    Not yet.
Just relax and it'll happen,
    no sweat.
Could it take another decade?
    You bet.

Marilyn L. Taylor

They will say, *How silly of me,*
   ho ho!
Will they add they're very sorry?
   Hell no.

Block That Trope

They used to flow so easily—the poems,
the syllables—like seed-pearls slipping down
a strand of disconnected chromosomes
for some unwritten sonnet. Every noun
would quickly find the quintessential verb
to lean against, quatrains would ebb and flow,
and nothing whatsoever would disturb
the equilibrium. Off they'd go
into that lyric wild blue yonder,
picking up some adjectives as needed,
working hard in tandem toward the wonder
of it all, sublimely unimpeded.
But nowadays—like pigeons on the wing—
disorder comes, and wrecks the whole damn thing.

III.

Outside the Frame: The Photographer's Last Letters to her Son

I. Wildwood Farm, April 3rd, 2017

Dear Nick,
      Well, it's starting over—April's
back debauching us again, the woods
are soaking wet, the mud dazzles, all
our stringy willow trees are going blond
and sentimental (just like the women
who write about them)—and I rise to the sight
of the grass nudging up green, brimming
with narcissi, practically overnight!
—Narcissi. From a distance, don't they look
like froth? Or whitecaps? Makes me want to run
away to sea—my sea, Nick. A maverick
ocean that doesn't move, but invites me in
to take its photograph, to document
its miracles. So this morning, in I went …

April 20th

It's my seventy-fifth April (sixty-fourth
with a camera in my hand) … and you wonder
why I desert my comfortable hearth
to crouch down on a patch of soggy tundra
taking pictures in the cold. Well, I'll
tell you why: it's to press my hands
against that rough young grass, to feel it yield
under my fingers, then to turn my lens
on the wetness underneath, where the soil
hides its buried treasure. Granite pearls,
flint sequins, limestone underpinnings—they're all
uncovered now, everything's exposed! The voyeur
in me goes feverish inside my head
watching seeds moving in their satin bed.

April 29th

… I'm cold today, Nicky. My jeans have two
black ovals in the front from where I knelt
to watch the moss, and it was well past noon
before I gave it up. (Everyone thought
I'd stayed too long; guess I'm getting old
and strange….) But where was I? Mice? No, moss.
The farmers used to call it "elfin gold"
because it only grows in crevices
and caves. It doesn't want the sun at all—
just what the sun leaves behind, the dwindling
evidence of light—something like the pall
that hovers around a burnt-out candle.
They found me humming, reading with my thumb
its little poem to the millennium.

II. Massachusetts General Hospital, May 22nd

In response to your rude questions
on the state of my health: I am of sound mind

and in my hands I hold the weight
of my soul, a leaden comfort

in my palm. Its polished crystal eye
opens, finds, fixes on the edges

of the enemy: a wall of grass,
leaves, stems and stalks, tangles

of roots and vines—the wild green Other
that follows me, no matter how

I slash and scythe my little path—
pursues me, even as I back away.

III. Roundtree Convalescent Home, October 2nd

I must compose	I must compose
myself, Nicky,	and focus the lens
and admit to you	for precise pinpoint
that I am terribly	focusing I must turn
frightened, the camera	the focusing ring until
has developed so many	the shimmering image
numbers and dials	becomes sharp I must
I forget what they	use fast shutter speeds
mean; its rings	to stop action stop
and buttons are all	action or I will produce
mixed up and when	a deliberate blur except
I finally try	for certain unusual
to take a shot all	lighting situations when
I see is parts	I must use the exposure
of my own eye	compensation dial to prevent
bristling with	over-exposure I must
daggers, staring	turn and turn until
back at me	the split image
grotesque and huge	becomes whole

IV. Wildwood Farm, January 25th

Obviously the FBI
has come to find hard
evidence of my
incompetence. They
think they're fooling me,
they even say I
have met them before,
but I have never
met them before, these
blond harpies who keep
asking me my name
and what day it is
today (*Up-yours-day?*)
and the exact where-
abouts of my gloves
and earmuffs,
the pinking shears,
the keys to the
boathouse, my Knirps
umbrella (as if I
needed one in winter!),
the pancake syrup,
the bottle of
cocktail onions,
the thumbtacks, the
remote control
TV channel changer,
extra extra pink
Pepto-Bismol,

Marilyn L. Taylor

some kitchen
safety matches
and a couple
of bowls of excellent
vanilla custard
from Christmas.

V. Roundtree Convalescent Home, February 4th

… whereas now I hold my hands
at arm's length and point
my index fingers skyward
and extend my thumbs
so that they meet tip to tip
thus making a frame (minus the top)

and with my frame I scan
the scenery; here a clump
of white buildings,
there a face, or a flower,
but so often nothing, Nicky—
nothing at all

Marilyn L. Taylor

VI. Roundtree, February 16th

The loud-talking
women are back
with their folding

table and their
jigsaw puzzle:
A Yorkshire Dale

showing part of
a hill and some
trees with huge holes

in them as if
a cannonball
had torn through their

upper reaches.
Try, the women
yell, *to find the*

*pieces. Look, here
is some sky!* But
it's hard, because

many are lost,
some are under
the table or

buried in the
cushions, a few
have been purloined—

slipped into the
untied bathrobe
of a hairless

geezer who says
he knows just where
the big tower

went and meanwhile in
our ears someone
croons *Would we like*

*to swing on a
star?* and at last
they wheel away

the puzzle and
bring another
in, dumping it

out and smiling—
as if to say
Maybe you won

that round, grandmaw,
but it's just
a matter of time.

Marilyn L. Taylor

VII. Roundtree, March 11th

All I know is that it's
about this big and I need it for
the things I do but
I can't remember
what's it's called. You put it
in the bigger thing
and it keeps it there
for you so when you want
to look at something later
there it is.
You know what I mean,
it's about so big
and it's not square,
it isn't square at all,
it's that other.
You have to use it
to make things stay where
they used to be
so you can take them out
and look at them where they were.
But God help me I
can't find it anywhere.
All I know for certain
is that it's about this big
and I need it, I need it very much.

VIII. Massachusetts General Hospital, March 30th, 2018

Have you come to say hello
maybe you will take me
I think it must be time
time to go now
goodbye

IX. Wildwood Farm, sometime in April

There are times each day
        when I go   off
                somewhere

when I return there is a little less of me
        as if each time
                one thread of mind
                        and memory
                    were pulled away

Soon I shall be   become
        entirely
                unraveled

I shall survive
        as
        afterimage
        as
          gatherer of light

After the Midnight Phone Call

does she still have to get
dressed, have to
put her shoes on,
tie them, run
a comb through
her hair   coat, coat

still have to
fumble for the
keys to the car,
shove them into
the ignition with
familiar scrape *money,
has she brought
any money?*

does she stop for
the red light
at a time like this
are the rules the
same, or are
dispensations made

will she get there
to find she's dreaming
the clock cranking back
the way it does in
the movies, and she
oh God
is really back in bed,

Marilyn L. Taylor

and will nobody be
bleeding, the heavy
doors of the hospital
never be opening
onto fluorescent
chaos and the end
of the world?

The Blue Water Buffalo

> PHNOM PENH, Jan. 28 2020—*Cambodia recorded 77 landmine and unexploded ordnance (UXO) casualties in 2019, up 33 percent compared with 58 in the year before.*
> —Xinhua News Agency

On both sides of the screaming highway, the world
is made of emerald silk—sumptuous bolts of it,
stitched by threads of water into cushions
that shimmer and float on the Mekong's munificent glut.

In between them plods the ancient buffalo—dark blue
in the steamy distance, and legless
where the surface of the ditch dissects
the body from its waterlogged supports below

or it might be a woman, up to her thighs
in the lukewarm ooze, bending at the waist
with the plain grace of habit, delving for weeds
in water that receives her wrist and forearm

as she feels for the alien stalk, the foreign blade
beneath that greenest of green coverlets
where brittle pods in their corroding skins
now shift, waiting to salt the fields with horror.

Marilyn L. Taylor

For Lucy, Who Came First

> *She simply settled down in one piece right where she was, in the sand of a long-vanished lake edge or stream—and died.*
> —Donald C. Johanson, paleoanthropologist

When I put my hand up to my face
I can trace her heavy jawbone and the sockets
of her eyes under my skin. And in the dark
I sometimes feel her trying to uncurl
from where she sank into mudbound sleep
on that soft and temporary shore

so staggeringly long ago, time
had not yet cut its straight line
through the tangle of the planet,
nor taken up the measured sweep
that stacks the days and seasons
into an ordered past.

But I can feel her stirring
in the core of me, trying to rise up
from the deep hollow where she fell—
wanting to prowl on long callused toes
to see what made that shadow move,
to face the creature in the dark thicket,
needing to know if this late-spreading dawn
will bring handfuls of berries, black
as blood, or the sting of snow,
or the steady slap of sand and weed
that wraps itself like fur
around the body.

Leaving the Clinic

Baja California, 1997

Having carried your own
terrible frailness
to the edge of the water

you bent your body sharply
like a broken stick, until
you were kneeling in the sand.

*If the world weren't so damned
beautiful,* you said, maybe
dying wouldn't be so bad—

But then you saw how a small rain
had pocked the creamy skin
of the beach overnight

causing snails to leave their sanctuaries,
and the pursed hibiscus buds
to fatten and explode,

and with the sea collapsing around us,
thinning to a glassy sheen
that blinded you

you hid your face
behind your hands and shook
with unrequited love.

Marilyn L. Taylor

What They Don't Know

They are thirteen, all flying elbows
and thinbone knees, wrapping their tongues
around words like *pimp* and *bare-ass*
and *hard-on*. They are astounded
by girls, the bodies of girls, the onrush
of lips and hair, and they talk about
what it would be like to touch one of those
flashy breasts, to look it in the eye.

They are thirteen, and they don't know
about the Buick they might be riding in
a year of two from now, packed in hip-to-hip
chanting a frenzied *go go go go*
until the pavement starts to bulge
and crest, lifting them, sending them up
into some kind of heartstop heaven.

They don't know that the tree might be an elm
that the car will wrap itself around
in lascivious embrace, or that afterwards
a thin, watery sigh *Open the door*
could be the first sound and the last
before sirens take up the threnody.

For now, though, they lean lightly
on their slender bikes, polishing
a new language: *horny, piss-off, kiss my ass.*
Expertly they palm their cigarettes,
the thick smoke streaming
from their mouths and noses.

Message from the Ice Cave

Received from a friend, newly widowed

I am living here now, where the cold
is my consort, the lover I clasp
with my arms and legs, from whose gray
blanket I tear each breath.

All around me ice is in bloom—
tiny glass buds keep swelling
from hairline fissures
in the stone. The buried river

cuts close, a dark ventricle
thick with sorrow. Moisture floods
my face, pools at my feet.
In time, a tower of ice

will grow around me, taking
the shape of an old woman
and visitors will say, *Look at her,
how she weeps into her hands.*

IV.

Reading the Obituaries

Now the Barbaras have begun to die,
trailing their older sisters to the grave,
the Shirleys, Helens, Nans—who said goodbye
just days ago, it seems, taking their leave
a step or two behind the hooded girls
who bloomed and withered with their century—
the Dorotheas, Eleanors and Pearls
now swaying on the edge of memory.
Soon, soon, the scythe will sweep for Jeanne
and Angela, Patricia and Diane—
pause, and return for Margie and Maxine
while Susan spends a sleepless night again.
   Ah, Lisa, how can you be growing old?
   Jennifer, Michelle, your hands are cold.

Marilyn L. Taylor

Late Spring, Early Fall

with apologies to Gerard Manley Hopkins

Margaret, are you gagging
since your body started sagging?
You can't believe the man who
so adored you dumped you, can you?
Ah! as your wrinkles burgeon
you recall that plastic surgeon
with his fake before-and-af-
ter photographs that made you laugh.
But it's different now. Not half
so comical. Unfair, in fact,
the way the deck is clearly stacked
against you. Why, you've never dreamt
of withering! You felt exempt.
But now? You fear what you love most
(especially Margaret) is toast.

Family Dynamic

Mel, Mel, the Dad from Hell
Raised your kids in a padded cell.
Not one soul cried the night you died,
But Mother giggled like a bride.

Marilyn L. Taylor

Women at Sixty

turn from their bodies
in embarrassment, as if
they had found themselves
wearing the wrong thing.
They wonder how
it could have come to this,
how the gardenia flesh
could have wilted on the stem
and how the boys they married
could be hovering like mayflies
around the wet-bar, learning
the slow idioms of old men.

They try to bring to mind
what they were doing
on the day growing old began:
opting for the condominium,
the artificial Christmas tree?
Catching their children speaking
in profundities? Or was it when
they first noticed, thunderstruck,
that their fickle bodies were
casually betraying them,
relentlessly eroding under
the damask of their skin?

It no longer takes them
by surprise, this revelation.
They have begun to understand
that they (of all people)
must finally slip into the role
of elder, of relic, of crone

and take their leave—gathering
their cloaks about them,
holding the edges tightly
at the throat.

Marilyn L. Taylor

Aunt Eudora's Harlequin Romance

She turns the bedlamp on. The book falls open
in her mottled hands, and while she reads
her mouth begins to quiver, forming words
like *Breathless. Promises. Elope.*
As she turns the leaves, Eudora's cheek
takes on a bit of bloom. Her frowzy hair
thickens and turns gold, her dim eyes clear,
the wattles vanish from her slender neck.
Her waist, emerging from its ring of flesh,
bends to the side. Breasts that used to hang
like pockets rise and ripen; her long legs
tremble. Her eyes close, she holds her breath—
the steamy pages flutter by, unread,
as lover after lover finds her bed.

The Seventy-Somethings in the Workshop

Breathless in their quilted overcoats
the silver-haired contingent now arrives,
shouldering their zippered canvas totes
stuffed with recent cuttings from their lives.

They claim they can't recall a single line
of poetry—but soon they're reeling off
entire chunks of Frost and Gertrude Stein,
Millay, MacLeish, Penn Warren, Nemerov—

and finally, from three-ring binders, lift
their own bespattered pages, creased and smudged
with fierce self-edits—like a sacred gift
to lay before the others, to be judged—

while Pound and Parker, Bishop and Jarrell
smile down upon them, wink, and wish them well.

Marilyn L. Taylor

The Tenth Avenue Care Home

> *Assisted living is a type of senior housing that allows elderly residents to lead more active, independent lives than they can in traditional nursing homes.*
> —www.assistedliving.com

We live in this house.
It fits right in.
Its windows face
the long afternoons.

It fits right in,
and no one would guess
the long afternoons
mean nothing to us

and no one would guess
that the other houses
mean nothing to us—
except for the little boys

that the other houses
gather in at dusk.
The little boys
think we're ghosts

gathering at dusk
to frequent their dreams.
They think we're ghosts
when our night visits seem

too frequent. Their dreams
make them shudder—
our night visits seem
like shadows, wavering but persistent.

Make them shutter
their windows, face
their own shadows. Wavering but persistent,
we live in this house.

Marilyn L. Taylor

Rondeau: Old Woman With Cat

Osteoporosis (one of life's indignities)
is such a splendid name for the disease—
all those little *o*'s, holes in the bone
where the rain gets in, rendering a crone
like me defective, porous as swiss cheese.

I'm riddled at the hips and knees,
roundsided as parentheses
since my shrunken spine has known
   osteoporosis—

and my extremities
have shriveled into lacy filigrees,
breakable as glass on stone.
Naked at the window ledge I drone
to my sleek, supple Siamese:
   osteoporosis.

Scaffolding

I have recently become aware
of the skull beneath my skin. The drapery
that covers it feels flimsy, papery
as birch bark—it will never re-adhere
to its familiar bony underlayer:
maxilla, frontal, nasal, every brace
that does the job of bolstering up my face
until the day it doesn't, leaving bare
a fierce, voracious grin, hollow stare,
socket-nose and nonexistent ears—
the omnipresent image that appears
on cans and plastic bottles everywhere
containing Drano, turpentine and lye—
a selfie, waiting for the day I die.

Marilyn L. Taylor

The Lovers at Eighty

Fluted light from the window finds her
sleepless in the double bed, her eyes

measuring the chevron angle his knees make
under the coverlet. She is trying to recall

the last time they made love. It must have been
in shadows like these, the morning his hands

took their final tour along her shoulders and down
over the pearls of her vertebrae

to the cool dunes of her hips, his fingers
executing solemn little figures

of farewell. Strange—it's not so much
the long engagement as the disengagement

of their bodies that fills the hollow
curve of memory behind her eyes—

how the moist, lovestrung delicacy
with which they let each other go

had made a sound like taffeta
while decades flowed across them like a veil.

We Real Old

after Gwendolyn Brooks' "We Real Cool"

The breakfast eaters:
Seven at the Golden Waffle

We real old. We
Catch cold. We

Take pills. We
Change wills. We

Can't hear. We
Crave beer. We

Eat prune. We
Die soon.

V.

Along the Brule

> *Of time you would make a stream upon whose bank*
> *you would sit and watch its flowing.*
> —Kahlil Gibran

Now I can watch the river.
Now, from this melting oxbow
where I sit with my senses steeping
in the sun, I am witness to the torrent,
but not yet of it.

Soon my perspective will be different.
I will be running with the groundwater
from grave to creek to roaring channel
where, among sticks and gravel
I will wash downstream with the other detritus,
remnants of what once was leaf, garden, gardener,

past the still-invisible piers and posts
of the next generation and the next and next
whose silver bridges
will one day arch, shimmering,
over the strange blue boats
of the remote unborn.

Marilyn L. Taylor

Extravaganza at Dave's

The house in this poem is not my house,
the red oaks arching over it not my trees—
but every time I come here, the birds
are glad to see me. They catch me spying on them
through the wide window and begin
to dance for joy—twirler, skyrocketer,
cartwheeler, prima ballerina, star performer
in the Cirque de Soleil of June.

Shirt-tail cousins, that's what they are—
related but distant, separable, each troupe
rehearsing its own routines and attitudes.
I watch them dive, then flutterup and catapult
for a sunflower seed—maintaining the careful
pecking order, the given choreography.
Through the screen, I hear the massed chorale
of the entire ensemble: *cardinal, jay,*
woodpecker, jay, robin, junco, bunting,
jay, jay, jay.

The Amazing Perseverance of the Sand-Hill Crane

Endangered species? Not this chick—she's got
a built-in arsenal: claw, bill, and feather,
and soon she'll pull her leggy act together,
gear up for the hunt. She'll troubleshoot
the dales and dunes where eligible males
from her subgenus are inclined to loiter,
then browse around, observe, and reconnoiter
until she's got her target by the tail.

Not for her, macaws that squall for freedom,
Not for her, the frowning peregrine;
She wouldn't know an albatross from Adam
and doesn't want some freckled featherbrain
puttering in the garden, spitting seeds.
One crane. One skinny crane. That's all she needs.

Marilyn L. Taylor

Summer Sapphics

Maybe things are better than we imagine
if a rubber inner-tube still can send us
drifting down a sinuous, tree-draped river
           like the Wisconsin—

far removed from spores of *Touristococcus*.
As we bob half-in and half-out of water
with our legs like tentacles, dangling limply
           under the surface

we are like invertebrate creatures, floating
on a cosmic droplet—a caravan of
giant-sized amoebas, without a clear-cut
           sense of direction.

It's as if we've started evolving backwards:
mammal, reptile, polliwog, protozoon—
toward that dark primordial soup we seem so
           eager to get to.

Funny, how warm water will whisper secrets
in its native language to every cell—yet
we, the aggregation, have just begun to
           fathom the gestures.

Still Lives

> *Many species ... can "hear" by detecting the vibrations of sound waves, without actually hearing the sound itself.*
> —Tutorial, Gallaudet University for the Deaf and Hard of Hearing, Washington, DC

This is for the tacit ones,
those creatures who have not
been wired for sound—
the snakes and armadillos, butterflies
and mollusks, worms and octopi
and my own white cat—
living out their lives
in the silence that is their lot,
oblivious to the speech of men,
loose shutters juddering in the wind,
squalls of rain backed by cadenzas
of thunder, and that five-note croon
of mourning doves who think nothing
of interrupting the hoot-owls
to bellow the blues.

Marilyn L. Taylor

Another Reason Never to Live North of 43 Degrees Latitude, Especially Near Lake Michigan

Summer around here doesn't leave
politely. No wafting away, full of good
excuses, into clouds of dissipating
humidity. No trailing nine o'clock sunsets
festooned with streamers the color
of seashells, or Damson plums.
Instead, she wakes up one morning
near the end of August, shakes the petals
out of her hair, takes a chilly look around,
and before we've had time to unplug the fan
and slam the windows shut, she's gone.
Just like that. Sometimes so fast
she catches her skirt in the door;
last year we were still finding shreds
as late as November.

Tackiest of Trees

with abject apologies to A. E. Housman

Tackiest of trees, the power poles
festooned with latticed rigmaroles
ascend our flowery hill like troops
of power-hungry nincompoops.

They speak a tongue not formed from leaves,
but from the buzzing in their sleeves
after a downpour, which converts
to hissy-fits in megahertz.

Something's ruthless in the look
of them, the zeal with which they wreck
the view—transforming countryside
to grid, forever uglified.

Marilyn L. Taylor

Drive All Night

Simply set your cruising speed at sixty-eight,
stick to the Interstate, and you'll arrive
like morning's minion, pal—your hair
wind-flattened on one side, pulse walloping
at optimum efficiency, tight schedule intact.
Just repeat after me: *avoid small towns.*

That's right, eschew those towns,
friend, those glomerations of eight
or nine hundred rubes named Dwayne, intact
in their dullness. Their collective aim: to arrive
at the local wienie-works on time—hair
greased, molars brushed, haunches walloping.

It's true, of course, that your own walloping
windshield wipers could turn some of these towns
(for all their Wal-Marts and parking meters and Hair
Chalets) into vapor-lit versions of eight-
eenth century streetscapes. Especially if you arrive
under canopies of ancient elms, all intact.

And if a row of bungalows, equally intact,
happens to feature one lace curtain walloping
crazily in the night breeze, you might arrive
at certain conclusions about small towns.
You might even come within a hair
of staying for supper. Even if you just ate.

Maybe you find a chrome diner, circa 1958,
with pictures of Charlie Chaplin tacked
to the walls. A waitress with long copper hair
grins and takes your order: a walloping

plate of beans and ham, followed by the town's
finest apple pie. Then the locals start to arrive:

> *Where's your girl, Dwayne? You got a rival, buddy? You just been eight-*
> *balled? Well, here's what the town's*
> *been saying—she ain't what you call intact,*
> *boy. Broad needs a good walloping*
> *to keep her zipped up and out of your hair.*

—Fade out. No diner, no copper hair, no small towns.
Only those walloping tires and the hum of your V-8.
Drive all night, friend. Arrive intact.

Marilyn L. Taylor

No Two Exactly Alike

Why have you closed yourself upstairs for hours
tending to a poem on this icy-moist, keen
April day? You and I could be outdoors
walking the woods, our boots leaving wet green
stains between the violets and paper-whites
still buried to their chins in snow—but no,
you've drifted up the stairs again to write
down still another simile for snow.

Snow Mist

A pseudonym for airborne slush,
it paves the Interstate with mush;
a drool of snowglops, cold and wet,
as beautiful as frozen sweat.
Drippings hang from sodden trees
and drop what looks like moldy cheese
or cultivated streams of snot
on every naked garden plot,
and solders to the drab cement
six clumps of doggie excrement.
It slimes the streets with greasy spray
till every car is charcoal-gray.
"Snow mist"? Right. A lovely call.
I call it crap, and that is all.

VI.

A Highly Caloric Lament

A pox upon you, Charlie's Chili Dogs,
T.G.I. Friday's, Coldstone Creamery,
you harpies of the dreaded calorie—
quit hitting on me till my judgment fogs,
and every vein and capillary clogs
with drippings from your latest recipe!
Arugula? Not for the likes of me,
and neither are those dreadful diet blogs.
Been there, done that—gave all my sweets away,
ate naked salad, kept the flab at bay.
But nowadays my magnitude increases.
I'm getting tubby. Fatter by the day.
Just look at me: mine aft has gang agley,
my life's in shreds, my mind's in Reese's Pieces.

Marilyn L. Taylor

Subject to Change

A reflection on my students

They are so beautiful, and so very young
they seem almost to glitter with perfection,
these creatures that I briefly move among.

I never get to stay with them for long,
but even so, I view them with affection:
they are so beautiful, and so very young.

Poised or clumsy, placid or high-strung,
they're expert in the art of introspection,
these creatures that I briefly move among—

And if their words don't quite trip off the tongue
consistently, with just the right inflection,
they remain beautiful. And very young.

Still, I have to tell myself it's wrong
to think of them as anything but fiction,
these creatures that I briefly move among—

Because, like me, they're traveling headlong
in that familiar, vertical direction
that coarsens beautiful, blackmails young,
and turns to phantoms those I move among.

Always Questions

> *Yesterday? At the mall? I bought a book of Emily Dickinson? For my mom?*
> —overheard at Starbucks

There is a moment, in the middle teens,
when virtually every sentence ends
on an upward curl, as if it really means
to be a question—or at least pretends

to entertain an element of doubt—
like this: *I started early? Took my dog?*
implying that I may have ventured out
exceptionally *late,* to take a jog

without the dog, or anyone else, along.
And if I add: *and visited the sea?—*
I'm hinting that of course I could be wrong
about this "sea" thing, ha-ha, you know me.

It's evidently hard for them to say
the thing they mean, without a little cue
for feedback, for the understood *Okay;*
or, possibly, they talk the way they do

because they are the representatives
of a long-out-of-date civility—
these gentle souls who speak in tentatives
and always dwell in possibility.

Marilyn L. Taylor

First Day in London

Notice how my voice has changed!
My vowels have broadened overnight;
Comes forth my syntax re-arranged
And all my *r*'s are out of sight.

I'll chat you up, I'll mind the gap,
I'll not forget my bumbershoot;
I'd love to stay till Boxing Day—
My haversack is in the boot!

Let's find a pub in Leicester Square;
We'll down a pint, or maybe two,
Then toss a busker half a quid
And lose it on the Bakerloo.

I know. I know. It's jolly clear
You'll never take me for a Brit—
My accent? Just a tribute band
That's longing for a cover hit.

Genesis

Just beyond the window casement
where I puttered in the basement
twenty-seven muddy nodes
were morphing into baby toads.

Wow, I shrieked in exaltation—
I am witness to creation!
Astonishing, without a doubt!
But even so, it grossed me out.

Marilyn L. Taylor

To My Neighbor John, Who Is Completely Happy

That moonlit warble in the summer dark
is you, John, singing your way home
from the Rehab Center where you work
evenings—one out-of-kilter chromosome
has never slowed you down. Your nightly whoop
floods the neighborhood with so much bliss
that my Dalmatian springs from sleep
and opens up her throat to harmonize
with you—along with every other canine
in a one-mile radius. Soon the air
is vibrating for blocks with strains
of an unearthly sweetness—prayers
rising from the bottom of the brain,
an ode to joy, with tabernacle choir.

For Max at Five Months

Hey, little handful,
beamish baby, super-napper,
better hold onto that smile—
there's a toddler hiding right behind you,
and only a moon or two away, a boy
with a book and a bike.

Can you guess
where they're headed?
Just around the corner, where
a young man stretched out on the grass
is contemplating a blue sky
filled with sailing ships.

As soon as you have learned
how to stand on your own
two feet you'll set off after them,
and one by one they will take
you in. You will grow more
and more invisible.

You won't even remember
being here, grinning at us
in pure, oblivious bliss—
where nothing interrupts
the present, or foreshadows
the great events to come.

Marilyn L. Taylor

Cecelia and Bobby: A Tale of Love Gone Wrong

At twenty years of age, Cecelia fled
her cozy bedroom in her father's house,
became her bashful boyfriend Bobby's spouse,
and plopped her body next to his in bed.

Ham-hocks in one hand, cupcakes in the other
she overdosed her Bobbykins with edible
delights—until he threw her out. Incredible?
He said it felt like bingeing with his mother.

The town's still talking after all these years
about the way Cecelia dried her tears,
and drove her little Subaru to Sears
to buy a set of barbecuing spears—

and how proficiently she did the job
of turning Bobby into Shish-ka-Bob.

Another Thing I Ought to Be Doing

> *Women should not fail to check their own breasts for suspicious lumps on a regular monthly basis.*
> —The American Cancer Society

So now I should be taking special care
of them, is that it? Every month go pat
pat pat—when what they've done for me is flat
out nothing? Zero? Case in point: where
were they when I was fourteen, fifteen,
and topographically a putting green?

Not to mention nights when I disgraced
my gender, stuffing tissue paper down
my polo shirt or confirmation gown—
my philosophy on staying chaste
having less to do with things profound
than fear of giving off a crunchy sound.

And now you're saying, *Minister to them!*
these very breasts that caused me great gymnasiums
of misery and high humiliation—
Institute a monthly regimen!
meaning I'm to "walk" my fingers gingerly
around these two molehills in front of me.

Sorry, but my hands have dropped straight down
like baby birds. They will not rise
to the occasion, won't get organized,
refuse to land on enemy terrain.
They simply twitch and fidget in my lap
as if they sense a booby trap—

Marilyn L. Taylor

As if they hear the moron in my head
insisting that I'll never be caught dead.

To a Cat Gone Blind in Her Nineteenth Summer

Every time you come back home to us
from one of your dazzling dreams,
a map of the known world unrolls
under the touchpads of your feet,
where shaggy broadloom prairie
gives way to the slick hinterlands
of linoleum and wooden floor.

You've opted for the great indoors,
a finite universe where cacophony
draws back: snarling Airedale is reduced
to spluttering fool, the power mower
rendered meek and harmless.
Even your fellow felines seem irrelevant,
being clearly otherwise engaged.

At the high window, a sparrow
is fretting. Your gaze swivels
smoothly in his direction and beyond,
as if you saw not only him, but also
his vestigial shadow (mercurial
in your mind's almond eye)
crossing a field of preposterous green
where it's April again and again.

Marilyn L. Taylor

The Turban

You look magnificent without your hair.
You look indomitable. You look proud
beneath the turquoise turban that you wear.

That turban doesn't tolerate despair—
no whiffs of what you'd never say out loud,
no mourning for your fallen chestnut hair.

Instead, you've taken on a feisty air
that never fails to captivate the crowd—
just like that winking turban that you wear.

She's bald! the turban cries. But you don't care;
it seems that you've entirely disavowed
all myths that claim you're less without your hair.

We see only your radiance up there,
more eloquent than kerchief, crown, or shroud,
out-glittering the turban that you wear—

which causes us to entertain a rare
surmise: something unearthly has endowed
you—and the turquoise turban that you wear—
with majesty. With or without your hair.

In Tanzania

Tonight I sleep
with the grass-eaters:
zebra and wildebeest
doze in clusters
near my tent, as moonlight
gathers in pools
over the high savannah.

Even under canvas I
am caught in a current
of dread as it eddies
past, ruffling mane
and beard. My herd
shudders as if one
creature, and listens.

Now the deep African sky
lifts a glittering claw;
we, the vulnerable, hear
the rasp of death
and twitch our haunches
as the golden cat
begins her dance.

Marilyn L. Taylor

The Odalisques

> *Images beamed to Earth from space have revealed that the moons of Uranus feature topographical oddities both baffling and bizarre.*
> —Astronomy Magazine, *December 6, 2016*

Here they come, the tiny tattered moons
of Uranus, their fluttering black chadors
still shrouding them, from the farthest rooms
of interplanetary space. The scars

of ancient fires are frozen on their faces,
faces ravaged by the labyrinth
of ragged rings and elemental gases
reeling about their icebound planet-prince.

Delivered now from their hermetic cells.
these elfin freaks—wounded and mortified—
permit us to draw back their heavy veils,
hear their frenzied whispers from the void.

The Gradual Unraveling of a Sycophant

Startling as it might seem, my deceit is
Starting to decompose. I find myself
Staring into the mirror, unable to
String along. I feel this bitter
Sting knowing that I must
Sing of my guilt, of the
Sin of being caught
In a vortex where
I now implode.

VII.

The Day after I Die

they will find the cure
for whatever got me,
and a unified theory
of physics will be announced
by a consortium
from M.I.T.

Following the funeral,
Earth will be contacted by
intelligent beings from
the Farquhar galaxy—
immediately after which
Tesla will announce a car
that can run forever
on table scraps.

Within the week,
Abbott Labs will introduce
an age-reversing cream
on the very heels of
a morning-after diet pill
that tastes exactly
like a Cadbury's Easter Egg.

Finally,
the woman they hire to clean
and fumigate my house
will come across a sheaf
of my old poems (tucked
optimistically inside a catalogue
from The Gap)

Marilyn L. Taylor

and turn them over to
her Thursday client, Billy Collins,
who (ignoring an infinitesimal twinge
of envy) will gallantly take charge
and see to everything—
including, of course,
any immortality.

Carpe Diem: A Quasi-Translation from the Latin

> *Carpe diem:* familiar phrase first used by the Roman poet Horace (ca. 35 BCE) to express the idea that one should enjoy life while one can.

Hold it right there, my superstitious friend—
don't waste your money on the zodiac
or sell the farm to some religious quack
to find out when your life is going to end.

It's obvious we're not supposed to know
if we've got one more winter left, or oodles.
So dry the dishes, go and walk the poodles—
the odds are good you'll live to see it snow.

And even if the surface of the sea
should rage the way it did when we were boys,
observing it from here or from the skies
makes not a shred of difference to the sea.

So pour yourself another glass of port
before your dithering becomes addictive.
Then smile, drink up, and keep Time in perspective.
Carpe diem, buddy. Life is short.

Marilyn L. Taylor

Notice from the Sweet Chariot Funeral Parlor

> *Due to predicted overcrowding in our cemeteries, a new service is available which will see to packing and storing one's remains in a space capsule for eventual launching into Earth's orbit.*
> —Discover Magazine

Dear Friend, we
    are operating at capacity
and cannot
    supply a green and grassy spot
for your tomb,
    as there is no more room.

Instead, you are invited to entrust
    your dust
to our space-age morticians, who seal
    in stainless steel
(thanks to post-Newtonian science)
    our clients.

Whereupon you
    (and all your shiny loved ones, too)
shall ascend
    via chartered rocketship, to spend
eternity
    very near where Heaven used to be.

Contingency

> *According to medical professionals, the minimum lethal dose of morphine is 200 milligrams, typically fourteen light blue 15 mg tablets. Unconsciousness usually occurs in 5 to 15 minutes, death in 20 to 50.*
> —Charles F. von Gunten, MD

As soon as the sun departs the house
At five in the afternoon
He deposits and seals in an amber jar
Another pale-blue moon.

He places the jar on the cabinet shelf
And swivels the handle tight;
Pockets the key in his terrycloth robe
And sits and waits for night.

He can hear the grandchildren crowing below,
Awash in their video games;
He tries for a time to assemble their faces,
And say a few of their names.

But he can't recall how many he has,
Or what their small fantasies are,
Or why their mothers and fathers have come
To put his clothes in the car.

He careens on the edge of a desperate thought,
A glimmer from where he's been—
But he doesn't remember the amber jar
Nor the moons crumbling within.

Marilyn L. Taylor

To the Mother of a Dead Marine

Your boy once touched me, yes. I knew you knew
when your wet, reddened gaze drilled into me,
groped through my clothes for signs, some residue
of him—some lusciousness of mine that he
had craved, that might have driven his desire
for things perilous, poisonous, out-of-bounds.
Could I have been the beast he rode to war?
The battle mounted in his sleep, the rounds
of ammunition draped like unblown blossoms
round his neck? Could I have somehow flung
myself against the wall of his obsessions,
leaving spells and curses on his tongue?
Your fingers tighten, ready to engage
the delicate hair-trigger of your rage.

At the End

In another time, a linen winding sheet
would already have been drawn
about her, the funeral drums by now

would have throbbed their dull tattoo
into the shadows writhing
behind the fire's eye

while a likeness
of her narrow torso, carved
and studded with obsidian

might have been passed from hand
to hand and rubbed against the bellies
of women with child

and a twist of her gray hair
been dipped in oil
and set alight, releasing the essence

of her life's elixir, pricking
the nostrils of her children
and her children's children

whose amber faces nod and shine
like a ring of lanterns
strung around her final flare—

but instead, she lives in this white room
gnawing on a plastic bracelet
as she is emptied, filled and emptied.

Marilyn L. Taylor

Poem for a 75th Birthday

for Allen Marcus Taylor, 1923–2012

Love of my life, it's nearly evening
and here you still are, slow-dancing
in your garden, folding and unfolding
like an enormous grasshopper in the waning
sun. Somehow you've turned our rectangle
of clammy clay into Southern California,
where lilacs and morning-glories mingle
with larkspur, ladyfern and zinnia—
all of them a little drunk on thundershowers
and the broth of newly fallen flowers.

I can't get over how the brightest blooms
seem to come reaching for your hand,
weaving their way across the loom
of your fingers, bending
toward the trellis of your body.
They sway on their skinny stems
like a gang of super-models
making fabulous displays of their dumb
and utter gratitude, as if they knew
they'd be birdseed if it weren't for you.

And yet they haven't got the slightest clue
about the future; they behave as if
you'll be there for them always, as if you
were the sun itself, brilliant enough
to keep them in the pink, or gold, or green
forever. Understandable, I decide
as I look at you out there—as I lean
in your direction, absolutely satisfied

that summer afternoon is all
there is, and night will never fall.

Marilyn L. Taylor

One by One

> *Nothing can cure the soul but the senses, just as nothing can cure the senses but the soul.*
> —Oscar Wilde

First, I'll press my hands against my ears
to silence the brass bands performing there
with frills and flourishes, greeting the years
as they sweep past. Instead, I will prepare
a quiet room for taking in the spare
continuo of leaves dropping from trees;
no harmonies are more profound than these.

Then I will draw backward from the stench
of living. I will make myself immune
to its erotic sweats and stinks, quench
my lust for one more August afternoon,
the steam of which will be forgotten soon—
the human brain is that incompetent
at conjuring the memory of scent.

Next, I must un-feel what I have felt
against the fingertip, the cheek, the groin—
that rare capacity we all were dealt
for knowing lavish pleasures, rattling pain,
lethal implosions where the two conjoin.
I un-remember them, I dis-evoke,
I let them dwindle into air and smoke.

Foreground, background. Particle and field.
Every law that proves or justifies
the separateness of things will be repealed:
Edges and shapes will melt before my eyes

till there is nothing left to recognize.
Blinking, I'll sit behind a watery scrim,
watching forms and colors seep and swim.

Last, I'll push aside the bedside glass
of medicated liquor, thick and sour,
refuse to let its chalk and brimstone pass
across my tongue. I yield, at this late hour,
reject the cloying aftertaste of power,
relinquish my compulsion to consume.
My shadow curls. I am the one consumed.

Marilyn L. Taylor

What Becomes of Us

We lived, we perished. Now we interweave,
we press together in these tangled spaces
dank with mold and liquefaction, cleave

to one another with our weedy faces
pressed against the soil, and cell by cell
we melt into the earth's beclotted places.

But soon the muck—enlivened by the swell
of us, our bygone selves—begins to spread
and undulate with curling, sensual

upheavals around a fallen seed,
a grain that's landed in the loamy green
vicinity of us. Something lies ahead.

Somewhere an outlaw gene,
furtively at first, will start to generate
an impulse that we couldn't have foreseen—

an overwhelming drive to procreate,
reproduce, multiply. And of necessity
we pull apart again and separate,

practicing the damp rituals of botany—
unfurling, reeking from the sod,
resplendent in our grand duality.

What becomes of us? We become God,
of course. Look up. How can we not believe,
not know that we are God?

Posthumous Instructions

After the fire, when I am rattling in my urn
and have no more to say to you, go home.
Have lunch. Ignore me, while I try to learn
the etiquette of ash and clinkerdom.

Let me settle. Let me reconcile
my boundaries with the cold geometry
of this strange vessel—my new domicile
whose curving contours reconfigure me.

Let me liberate the elements
that fused in me the morning I was formed
and offer them again, as evidence
that my short visit left this place unharmed.

Help me be part of what the earth reclaims
when you return to scatter my remains.

Marilyn L. Taylor

Glimmers in a Time of Peril

Wait! A miracle could happen here.
Just look at the moon—is it turning blue
tonight? And can it possibly be true
that's not an ambulance you hear out there,
but the fat lady singing, loud and clear?
Could the cows (woefully overdue)
be coming home at last? I challenge you
to deny a sudden sweetness in the air.

On the other hand, it's understood
that if we dream too soon about reviving
our forsaken, sickly planet on a tide
of hope, we cut our chances of surviving.
Yet how can we deny that something good,
however inconceivable, is thriving?

Acknowledgments

I am grateful to the editors of the following journals where some of the poems in this collection originally appeared (occasionally in earlier versions).

American Life in Poetry: "Home Again, Home Again"
The American Scholar: "Rondeau: Old Woman with Cat"
The Atlanta Review: "In Defense of the Much-Maligned Spondee"
Dogwood Journal: "Notes from the Good-Girl Chronicles, 1963"
The Formalist: "The Amazing Perseverance of the Sandhill Crane," "First Day in London"
Free Verse: "Contingency"
GSU Review: "Reading the Obituaries"
Indiana Review: "The Lovers at Eighty," "Drive All Night"
Iris: "To Lucy, Who Came First"
Journal of the American Medical Association: "Another Thing I Ought to Be Doing"
Light: A Journal of Light Verse: "Tackiest of Trees," "The Four Who Would Be Will," "Snow Mist," "Drinking with Dylan Thomas"
Measure: "Always Questions"
Poemeleon: "The Aging Huntress Speaks to Her Reflection," "Agnostic's Villanelle," "The Blue Water Buffalo," "To My Neighbor John, Who Is Completely Happy"
Poet Lore: "What They Don't Know"
Poetry: "Summer Sapphics," "Poem for a 75th Birthday," "The Geniuses Among Us," "Subject to Change"
Raintown Review: "Aunt Eudora's Harlequin Romance," "Notice from the Sweet Chariot Funeral Parlor"
Re/Verse: "Mel, Mel" (originally titled "Family Dynamic")
Smartish Pace: "To a Cat Gone Blind in Her Nineteenth Summer," "To the Mother of a Dead Marine"
Southern California Anthology: "Outside the Frame"
Umbrella: "In Other News"
Valparaiso Literary Review: "Crickets: A Late Chorale"
Verse Wisconsin: "Piano Overture"
Wisconsin Poets' Calendar, 2010: "Another Reason Never to Live North of 43 Degrees Latitude"

About the Author

MARILYN L. TAYLOR, former Poet Laureate of the state of Wisconsin and the city of Milwaukee, is the author of seven previous poetry collections. Her work has also appeared in *Able Muse, Measure, Poetry, Light, Raintown Review* and *Rhino,* among many other journals and anthologies. She has been awarded the Margaret Reid Poetry Prize for formal verse, and was a finalist for the X. J. Kennedy Parody Prize, the Howard Nemerov Sonnet Award, the *Lascaux Review* prize, the 2021 Maria W. Faust Sonnet Contest, and the 2021 *Able Muse* Write Prize. She serves as Associate Editor for two poetry journals, *Verse-Virtual* and *Third Wednesday*. For more about her, please visit **mltpoet.com**.